LEARN THE VALUE OF

Faith

◆

by ELAINE P. GOLEY

Illustrated by Karen Park

◆

ROURKE ENTERPRISES, INC.
VERO BEACH, FL 32964

Library of Congress Cataloging-in-Publication Data

Goley, Elaine P., 1949–
    Learn the value of faith.

    Summary: Examines the meaning of faith and gives
examples that illustrate its importance in day-to-day life.
    1. Confidence—Juvenile literature.   [1. Faith.
2. Confidence.]   I. Title. II. Title: Faith.
BJ1533.C6G64   1988   179′.9—dc19   88-35306
ISBN 0-86592-386-8

Faith

Do you know what **faith** is?

Faith is knowing that your friends will be
true to you...no matter what.

Your parents have **faith** in you... They know you can do well in math.

We have **faith** in the policeman who helps us when we're lost.

Knowing that your family loves you very much,
is having **faith** in them.

Faith is knowing the doctor can help you get better when you're sick.

You have **faith** in your baseball team because
you believe they can win.

Faith is knowing that your parents will always
be there when you need them.

We have **faith** in the President and Congress…
We believe in their ability to lead our country.

Your neighbor asks you to babysit for her children because she has **faith** that you are a responsible person.

The Pilgrims had **faith** in the future of our nation when they celebrated the first Thanksgiving.

Your dog has **faith** in you because he knows
you are responsible enough to walk him
and feed him every day.

When you know you can learn to play a piano piece well, you have **faith** in your own ability.

Faith is knowing a flower seed will grow when you plant it and water it.

K. Park

Knowing that the Creator put us on earth for a very special reason, is having **faith**.

Your teacher has **faith** in your ability to write a story in class.

Seeing a bird in the snow gives us **faith** that
spring will come again.

29

Faith is believing in yourself and others.

Faith

"I know you kids can really play baseball,"
said the coach. "We lost a game, but I
don't want you to be discouraged. Team spirit,
trying hard, and being good sportsmen are
more important than winning."

When Tom got home, his mother said, "Tom,
what's wrong? I can see that you're upset."

"We lost a baseball game today, Mom."

"Don't worry about it, Tom," said his mother.

"I'll bake some brownies for the team's
next game and we'll have a party, win or lose.
You and your sister can make a banner to
show the team we think they're great."

Tom and his sister made a large sign that said:
"GO TIGERS!"

How did the coach show the team that he
had **faith** in them?

How did Tom's mother show her **faith** in him?

How can you show someone that you have **faith**
in him?

Faith

One day, Miss Simmons said, "Paul,
I'd like to speak to you after class."

When class was over and the other students
left the room, she said, "Your homework paper
was not well written, Paul. It was messy
and poorly done. It is not up to your usual
good work. I know you can do better.
Please do it over tonight and bring it to me
in the morning."

"Yes Miss Simmons," said Paul.

When he got home, Paul said, "Mom, will
you help me do my homework over? I think I can
do it right this time."

Paul's mother said, "I know you can
do better, too."

How did Miss Simmons show that she had
faith in Paul?

How did Paul have **faith** in himself?

How did Paul's mother show her **faith** in him?